Traditional Crafts from
CHINA

Traditional Crafts from
CHINA

by Florence Temko

with illustrations by Randall Gooch

Lerner Publications Company • Minneapolis

*To Rachel, Perri, David, Dennis, Janet,
Tyler, and Yolanda, and for our wish for
international peace and friendship.*

Over the years, I have tucked away bits of information in my files
that have contributed to my fascination with crafts. They were
gathered mainly from personal meetings, books, magazines,
libraries, and museums in the United States and abroad. I regret
it is no longer possible to disentangle these many and varied
resources, but I would like to acknowledge gratefully and humbly
everyone who has helped to make this book possible.

—Florence Temko

Lerner Publications Company
A division of Lerner Publishing Group
241 First Avenue North
Minneapolis, MN 55401 U.S.A.

Website address: www.lernerbooks.com

Library of Congress Cataloging-in-Publication Data

Temko, Florence
    Traditional crafts from China / by Florence Temko ; with illustrations by
Randall Gooch.
        p.   cm. — (Culture crafts)
    Includes bibliographical references and index.
    Summary: Explains the meaning of Chinese culture which is found in eight
traditional handicrafts and provides instructions for creating them. Includes a
list of materials needed.
    ISBN 0-8225-2939-4 (lib. bdg. : alk. paper)
    1. Handicraft—China—Juvenile literature. [1. Handicraft—China.] I. Gooch,
Randall, ill. II. Title. III. Series.
TT101.T437 2001
745'.0951—dc21   99-050692

Manufactured in the United States of America
1 2 3 4 5 6 – JR – 06 05 04 03 02 01

CONTENTS

WHAT ARE CRAFTS?

All over the world, people need baskets, bowls, clothes, and tools. In modern times, people make many of these things in factories. But long ago, people made what they needed by hand. They formed clay and metal pots for cooking. They wove cloth to wear. They made baskets to carry food. We call these things "crafts" when they are made by hand

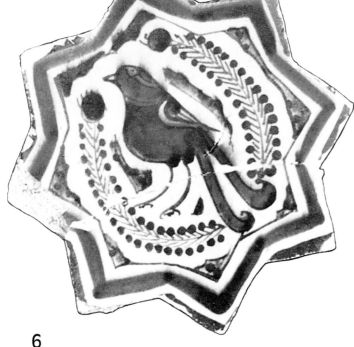

Grandparents and parents taught children how to make crafts. While they worked, the elders told stories. These stories told of their family's culture—all of the ideas and customs that a group of people believe in and practice. Children learned these stories as they learned the ways of making crafts. They painted or carved symbols from those stories on their crafts.

6

Year after year, methods and symbols were passed from parents to children. Still, each bowl or basket they made would look a little different. A craft made by hand—even by the same person—never turns out the exact same way twice.

People who are very good at making crafts are called artisans. Many artisans still use the old methods. They make useful things for themselves and their homes. Some artisans also sell their crafts to earn money.

Left to right: A painted tile from Turkey, a Pueblo Indian pitcher, a pot from Peru, and a porcelain dish from China

MATERIALS AND SUPPLIES

Some of the suggested materials for the crafts in this book are the same as those used by Chinese artisans. Others will give you almost the same results. Most materials can be found at home or purchased at local stores. Check your telephone book for stores in your area that sell art materials, craft supplies, and teachers' supplies. Whenever you can, try to use recyclable materials—and remember to reuse or recycle the scraps from your projects.

MEASUREMENTS

Sizes are given in inches. If you prefer to use the metric system, you can use the conversion chart on page 58. Because fractions can be hard to work with, round all metric measurements to the nearest whole number.

FINISHES

The crafts in this book that are made from paper will last longer if you brush or sponge them with a thin coat of finish. These are some choices:

White glue (Elmer's or another brand) is the most widely available. Use it at full strength or dilute it with a few drops of water. Apply it with a brush or small sponge. (The sponge should be thrown away after you use it.) White glue dries clear.

Acrylic medium is sold in art supply stores. It handles much like white glue. You can choose a glossy (shiny) finish or a matte (dull) finish.

CHINESE CRAFTS

The People's Republic of China occupies most of eastern Asia. Three arms of the Pacific Ocean—the Yellow Sea, the East China Sea, and the South China Sea—border China's eastern coast. Other Asian nations surround China to the north, west, and south.

China has the oldest recorded culture in the world. Scientists have discovered human bones dating back half a million years and written records dating to the 1700s B.C. Throughout this history, Chinese people have made different kinds of crafts according to the different natural resources of their regions. In some places, people discovered deposits of clay. They dug up supplies to make pots and other containers. Artists also made clay into sculptures. Early potters molded their crafts by hand, but by the A.D. 900s, Chinese people made porcelain dishes on potter's wheels.

Since ancient times, Chinese women have woven silk. They used silk cloth and thread to make clothing and beautiful embroidery. Chinese scholars and artists also used silk—or thin strips of bamboo—as a material on which to write or paint. The Chinese later invented paper, which was cheaper and easier to write on. In time, people turned paper into a craft material of its own.

In modern times, Chinese factories produce crafts, including embroideries, toys, ceramics, and paper crafts. But the Chinese government supports arts and crafts centers to encourage people to use and teach the age-old handcrafting methods.

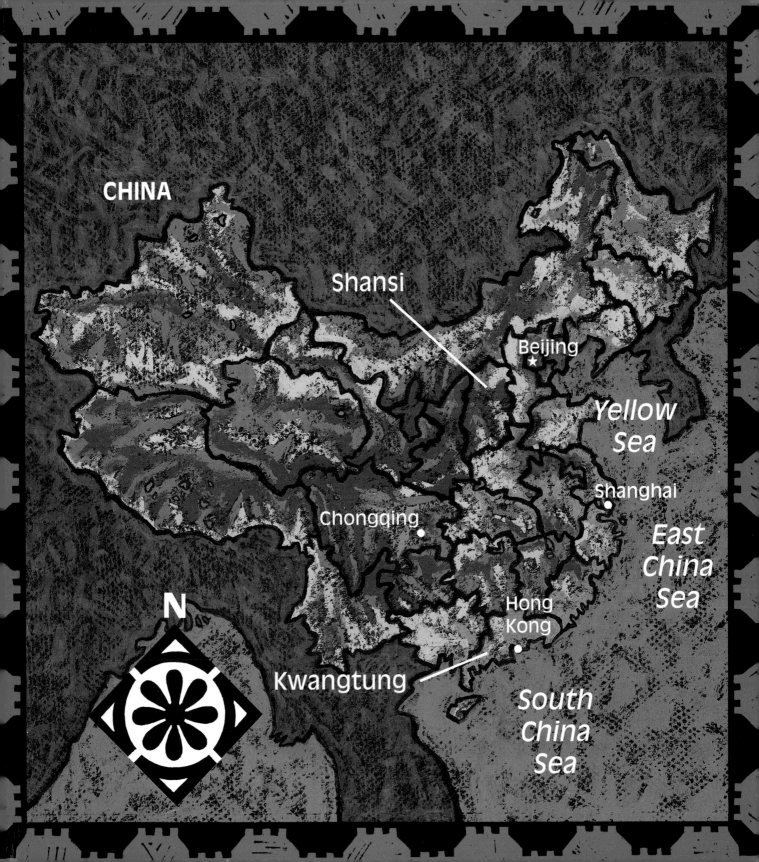

Paper Cutouts

Cutouts can be simple, such as the leaf and the dragon, or more difficult, such as the rooster and the round symbol.

CUT PAPER DECORATIONS

For at least 1,500 years, Chinese people have cut paper into pictures of flowers, animals, or scenes from everyday life. They paste their cutouts to walls, ceilings, and windows. In the past, many rural homes had windows covered with oiled paper. During the day, people inside the house could see cutouts pasted to the windows. At night, when the room was lit, passersby could see the figures from the outside, too.

A woman in Beijing attaches a new paper cutout to her window.

Styles of paper cutting vary from region to region. Folk artists in the northern province of Shansi (SHAHN-SEE) create bold designs. Those in the eastern province of Chekiang (zhu-zhee-AHN^g) make delicate, lacelike designs. Cutters in Kwangtung (GWAHN^g-DUN^g) specialize in multicolored pictures. They glue small pieces of tissue paper to the backs of shiny foil cutouts.

Paper cutters are at their busiest around the time of the New Year Festival, which comes between late January and mid-February. Before the holiday, families clean their homes and replace old, tattered cutouts with new ones.

TECHNIQUE

At home, Chinese people cut their own favorite decorations with scissors. They may draw a rough sketch on the back of the paper or cut freehand. Professional paper cutters use knives that they make themselves. They attach straight or round blades to bamboo handles. An artisan places a stencil on top of a pile of many papers and guides a knife straight down into the stack.

HOW-TO PROJECT

Chinese paper cutters use tissue paper, but colored bond paper and origami squares are easier to handle. When cutting curves, turn the paper to meet the scissors. The hand holding the scissors should remain in the same position.

> ### You need:
>
> Paper in two contrasting colors
> Pencil or photocopy machine
> Scissors
> White glue

1 Trace or photocopy a pattern from page 57 onto a piece of colored paper. First cut the outline. To reach the inside areas, cut a slit from the arrow. (Later, when you glue down the cutout, the slits will disappear.)

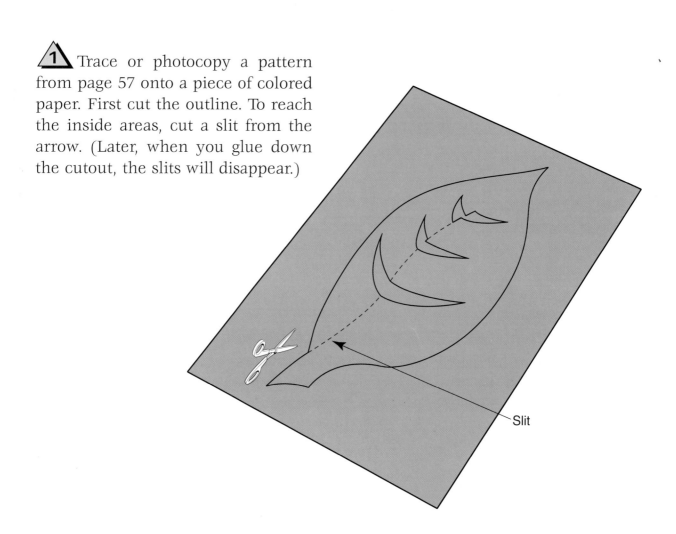

Slit

2 Glue down the cutout, using as little glue as possible. Otherwise the paper may buckle. Place the cutout on a piece of paper. Then put a blob of glue on a piece of scrap paper. With the forefinger of one hand, hold down the center of the cutout. Dip your other forefinger into the glue. With the thumb of the first hand, lift a section of the cutout. Smear some glue on the back.

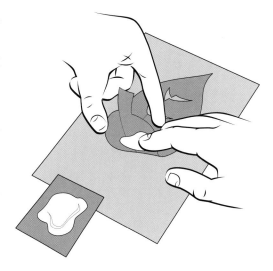

3 Repeat this on other areas until the whole cutout is pasted down. For any slits you used to make inside cuts, push the edges close together so that the slit is no longer visible. Pat down all over the paper.

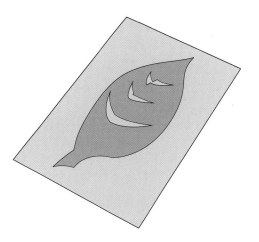

WHAT ELSE YOU CAN DO

Raised Pictures: When you glue cutouts on a background, they may look as though they are painted. To show that they are cut from paper, you can raise them so that they throw a slight shadow. Instead of gluing the cutout, stick tiny squares of two-sided foam tape—or small pieces of cotton dipped in glue—behind the cutout at several points.

Dough Clay Figures

Dough clay is easy to make and fun to use.

DOUGH CLAY

Chinese boys and girls like to play with toy tigers, snakes, and peacocks. Children form these figures with clay made of flour and salt. The material is called dough clay because the same ingredients go into bread. The dough can be worked just like clay that comes from the earth.

Chinese people can also buy dough clay figures from artisans. These skilled crafters travel from

An artisan paints a dough clay figure he has made to sell at a festival.

village to village, set up shop for a day or two, and then move on.

TECHNIQUE

Artisans who work with dough clay mix the ingredients together and knead them like bread dough. Crafters shape the dough into whatever they choose—perhaps a lion, a panda, a fan, or a flower. They let the figures dry in the open air or bake them in an oven until they are hard. Finally they paint the toys with bright colors.

The panda is China's favorite animal. Pandas have been around for two million years, but in modern times they are an endangered species. In the wild, they live only in protected areas in the mountains of China, where they feed on bamboo shoots and leaves. On this diet, pandas grow into adults about 6 feet tall, weighing 300 pounds.

HOW-TO PROJECT

You can make a panda from dough clay. When you join the parts, make small dents on the figure where pieces are to be attached. Wet the two places with a finger dipped in water. Smooth over the joint with your wet finger.

Caution: Dough clay dries out quickly. Cover the unused portion with a wet paper towel as you work.

You need:

Old newspaper
Medium size bowl
1 cup all-purpose flour
½ cup salt
Fork
½ cup hot water
Baking sheet (optional)
Pot holder (optional)
Narrow brush
Tempera or acrylic paints in white and black
Green marker
White glue

1 Cover your work area with newspaper. In the bowl, mix the flour and salt with a fork. Add the hot water gradually, stirring between each addition. You may not need all the water, but add enough so that the mixture is crumbly and begins to stick together.

2 Take the dough out of the bowl and mash it over and over with both hands until it is well mixed and becomes stretchy. This is called kneading. If the dough is too stiff, add a few drops of water. If it is too wet, add more flour.

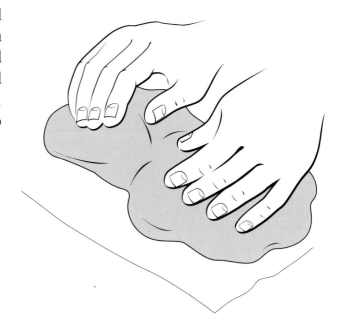

3 For the panda's body, roll some dough into a ball about 1³/₄ inches across. Roll a smaller ball for the head. Roll small balls for the ears and legs. Roll sausages for the arms. Shape them to be more lifelike. Moisten the parts that will be joined, then put the panda together.

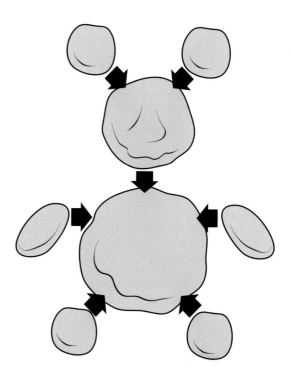

4 Leave the figure to dry in the air for about two days. With the help of an adult, you can speed up the drying by setting the panda on a cookie sheet and baking it in a 250°F oven for about three hours. Use a pot holder to handle the hot baking sheet. Allow the figure to cool completely before decorating.

5 Paint the panda white all over. Let it dry. Paint the black parts and let dry. Draw some green bamboo.

△6 Let the panda dry thoroughly for a few days. Then cover it with two coats of white glue to preserve it. The salt in the dough attracts moisture, and an uncoated dough clay figure may become sticky after awhile.

WHAT ELSE YOU CAN DO

Zodiac Animals: Chinese people name each year after one of the 12 different animals of their zodiac. The zodiac animals, in order, are the rat, ox, tiger, rabbit, dragon, snake, horse, goat, monkey, rooster, dog, and bear. Chinese people believe that the year—and the people born during it—will have some of the characteristics of its name animal. You can make a dough clay figure for your animal year.

Experiment with Tools: Use the back of a spoon to smooth your figures. Make lines with a toothpick or a fork. For hair, squeeze some dough through a garlic press.

Keeping Dough Clay: You can keep extra dough in a plastic bag in the refrigerator for a few days.

Kites

You can decorate your kite with a dragon or any other design you like.

KITES

Chinese people have flown kites since as long ago as 2600 B.C. People flew kites not only for fun, but also because they were useful. Soldiers flew kites to signal each other from far away. Farmers flew kites over fields to scare away birds. Most modern kites are for entertainment.

TECHNIQUE

In the earliest days, kite makers covered wooden frames with silk. Modern craftspeople are more likely to use paper, cotton, Tyvek (a paperlike plastic), or nylon parachute fabric. Besides traditional rectangular or six-sided shapes, Chinese kite makers create designs that look like birds, dragons, insects, and other flying things. They decorate the

Chinese children and adults gather at a town square to fly kites on a windy day.

In Chinese folklore, dragons are powerful, friendly water spirits. Dragons bring the rain and river water that farmers need to grow crops. Chinese dragons take many forms in illustrations and on cloth patterns, but only members of the emperor's household were allowed to use a dragon with five claws.

kites with bold pictures in brilliant colors that can still be seen at great heights. Most kites need the weight of a tail to keep them from spinning. For the last step, kite makers attach a loop of string called a bridle to the sides of each kite. The bridle is the place to tie on the long flying line (the string used to fly the kite).

HOW-TO PROJECT

The instructions show how to make a six-sided kite. Besides the suggestions in the list to the right, you can use any kind of lightweight paper, such as a colored page from the newspaper, tissue paper (although this tears easily), or Tyvek (sold in home supply stores). Many toy stores and any kite store sell kite string on a spool. If you wish, you can wind string around a smooth stick or the cardboard tube from a roll of toilet paper.

You need:

Old newspaper
Butcher paper, banner paper, or
   gift wrap
Scissors
Ruler
Pencil
Colored markers
A 36-inch dowel, ⅛ inch thick
Tape
Pin
100 to 200 feet thin string
Smooth stick or cardboard tube

1 Spread old newspaper over your work surface. Cut a piece of paper 18 inches by 30 inches and fold it in half. Draw on and cut the pattern shown in the diagram.

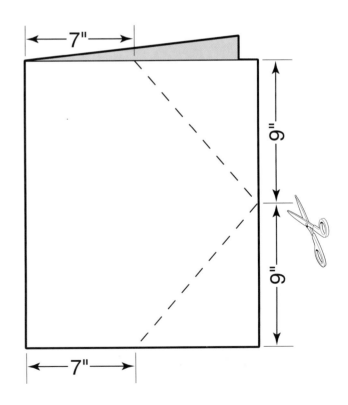

2 Unfold the paper. Decorate one side with markers. If the paper curls up and won't lie flat, you can weigh the corners down while you draw.

3 Cut the dowel into two pieces, each 18 inches long. Tape them on the plain side of the kite at the top and bottom and at three places in the middle.

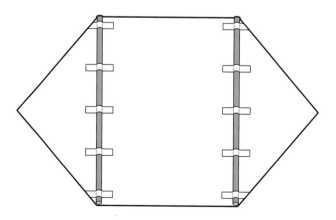

4 Stick pieces of tape on the front of each side corner. Then use a pin to pierce two holes through each corner. Cut a piece of string 4 feet long. Knot the ends through the holes. Put another piece of tape over the back of each pair of holes. This string is the kite's bridle.

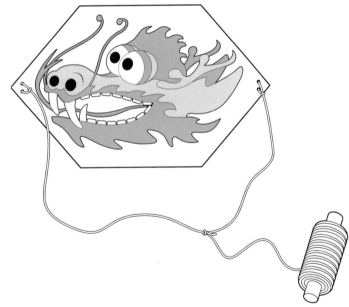

5 For the flying line, wind the rest of the string around the stick or cardboard tube. Tie the free end of the flying line to the middle of the bridle.

How to fly your kite:

This kite requires only a light breeze to fly well. Turn your back to the wind. With one hand, hold the kite by the bridle. Hold the flying line in the other hand. Lift the kite up high. When you feel the kite catch the wind, let it go with a slight upward toss away from you. Gradually reel out as much string as needed.

If the kite does not go up on the first attempt, then try again. To help the kite get started, hold it up while running into the breeze.

WHAT ELSE YOU CAN DO

Tail: This kite flies well without a tail, but it may fly even better if you staple some tissue paper strips near the bottom of the dowels.

Contests: Every September 9, Chinese people celebrate a kite-flying festival. Kite fighting is one of the main events. Fancy stunt kites perform acrobatic flights at high speed. Kite fighters glue ground glass to their kite strings and try to cut the lines of other flyers' kites. You can hold a kite-flying festival on September 9 or on any other day. Give prizes for the largest kite, the smallest, the one that stays up the longest, or the most beautifully decorated one.

String Puppets

You can make a puppet that looks like a Chinese princess (top) or scholar (right) from ancient times, a soldier (bottom), or a farmer (left).

PUPPETS

Performing stage plays with puppets is a popular Chinese tradition. For hundreds of years, puppeteers have traveled from village to village. The audiences usually already know how the play's story will go. Even so, people enjoy seeing them again and again.

This puppet has jointed arms and hands. The puppeteer moves each part with a separate string.

TECHNIQUE

Chinese puppeteers carve their figures from wood. The puppeteer moves the puppets with strings attached to wooden crossbars. An experienced puppeteer can make the figures perform many actions. The puppets might appear to be walking, climbing mountains, or dancing.

One very popular puppet play, *Journey to the West*, is adapted from a famous Chinese book. The story is based on the real journey of a monk who traveled from India to China in the 700s. The main character, Sun Wukong, is also called the Monkey King. As Sun Wukong and his friends travel over rugged mountains and dry deserts, they meet many criminals in disguise. Sun Wukong fights fierce battles to overcome evildoers. He also loves to play tricks on people.

HOW-TO PROJECT

Make a simple cardboard puppet that can be worked with two strings. If you use fishing line, an audience will not be able to see the strings.

You need:

Light cardboard or cereal box
Scissors
Crayons, markers, or poster
   paints
Needle with a wide eye
Thread or light fishing line
Tape
3 pennies, paper clips, or other
   weights

1 Cut the cardboard into one 3-inch by 5-inch piece for the puppet's body and two 1-inch by 2½-inch pieces for the arms. Draw the face and clothing. Cut out the puppet if you like.

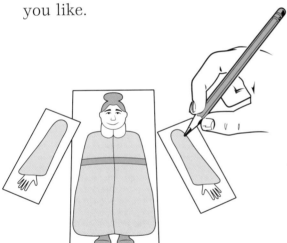

2 With the needle, pierce holes through the arms and body at the shoulders. Sew the arms loosely to the body with needle and thread. Knot the ends of the thread together.

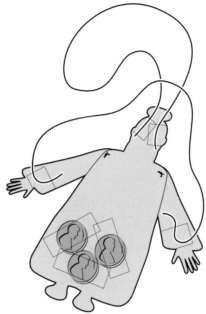

3 Cut a piece of thread about a foot long. Tape one end to the back of each of the puppet's arms. Tape another loop of thread to the back of the head. Tape three pennies or other weights to the back near the bottom of the puppet.

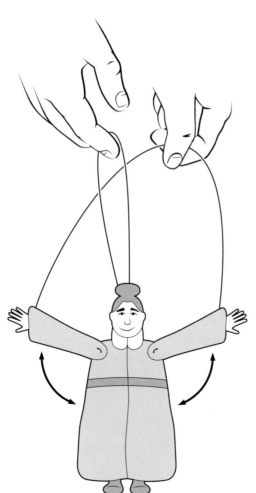

4 Hold the head string in one hand and the arm loop in the other hand. You can adjust the length of the loops by winding some of the thread around your fingers. Rest the bottom of the puppet on a flat surface, such as a low tabletop. Raise and lower the head loop to make the puppet bow and walk. Tug on either side of the arm loop to make the puppet move its arms.

Tangrams

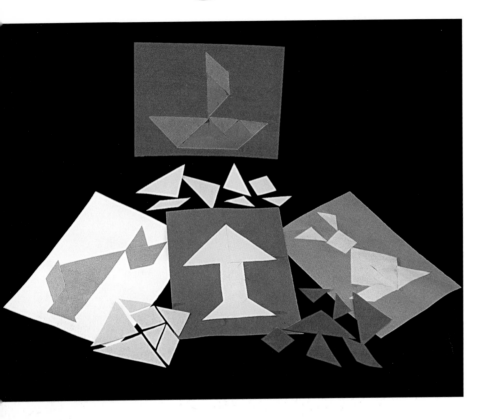

Some tangram pictures you can make are a sailboat (top), a cat (bottom left), a lamp (bottom center), and a rabbit (bottom right).

TANGRAM PUZZLES

An ancient Chinese puzzle called a tangram is a square cut into seven pieces. People arrange their tangrams into pictures and challenge others to make the pictures. The game may have been created when someone accidentally broke a square tile into seven pieces and formed them into a house, a boat, or an animal. Since then, children and adults all over the world have arranged tangrams into hundreds of different designs.

Two Chinese girls work a sheet of tangram puzzles (right). The sheet shows the solid outlines of the puzzles. The girls try to make the pictures with their pieces. The sheet also shows the solutions for tangram pictures such as this tugboat (above right) and this cat (above left).

HOW-TO PROJECT

It's very simple to cut tangrams from any kind of sturdy paper. The fun is in playing with the seven pieces.

1 Photocopy the pattern at right, enlarging the picture to the size you like. Or use a pencil and ruler to draw a square (5 to 7 inches is a good size). Then mark the lines as shown.

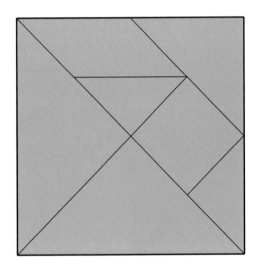

2 Cut the square apart at the lines.

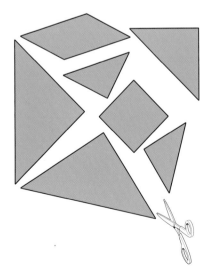

3 Use your tangram to create pictures, always using all seven pieces. Try to copy the patterns on page 56. You can also play with the pieces until you have come up with a picture. Or you can decide beforehand to make something specific.

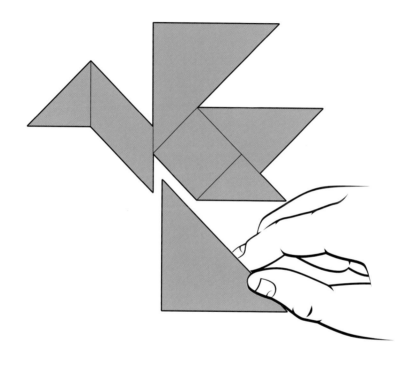

WHAT ELSE YOU CAN DO

Games: Challenge your friends to a game of tangrams.

1. Prepare the bird pattern and ask your friends to copy it with their pieces.

2. Show your friends only the outline for the rabbit and set a time limit for completing it with their pieces.

Needlework Purse

You'll apply the basic skills of embroidery when you make these colorful purses.

EMBROIDERY

For centuries Chinese women and girls have practiced a type of needlework called embroidery. In the past, a girl learned simple stitches when she was about eight years old. By the time she grew up, she was an expert. She used her skill to decorate such things as clothing, pillowcases, slippers, and headwear for herself and her family.

Two embroiderers stitch panels of traditional Chinese pictures in a workshop in Ch'eng-tu, a city in south central China.

TECHNIQUE

A needleworker may either draw a pattern directly on the fabric or place a paper stencil on top. She stretches a portion of the fabric on a frame and begins stitching. The embroiderer uses different stitches to show different textures. As she completes one part of the work, she stretches another section of the fabric on the frame. The drawn-on pattern or paper gradually disappears from view as the embroiderer completely covers it with stitches.

HOW-TO PROJECT

The directions show how to stitch a purse on plastic canvas, which is easier to work with than fabric. This project is for beginners, but it may take several hours to finish.

How to start a row

Always begin your stitch from the back of the canvas. Pull the yarn to the front, leaving about an inch at the back. As you work, catch the short length of yarn in your first few stitches to hold it in place on the back of the canvas.

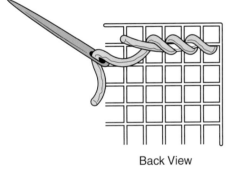

Back View

You need:

A piece of 7-mesh plastic canvas, 19 squares wide and 45 squares tall
Ruler
Marker
Photocopy machine or tracing paper
Stapler
One skein of worsted weight acrylic yarn in each of three colors (for example, dark blue, pink, and light green)
Tapestry needle
Scissors
1 large snap fastener
A 2-inch square of cardboard

How to do a running stitch

Running stitches are used to outline a pattern. Poke the needle up through the back of the canvas at point 2. Sew down at point 1. Come up again at 3. Sew down at point 2. Continue along the outline, moving forward with an up stitch and sewing back down into the previous stitch.

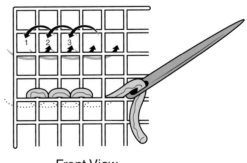

Front View

How to do a slant stitch

Slant stitches are used to fill in large areas. Begin stitching on the left side of your sewing area. Starting at square 1, push the needle up through the canvas. Sew down into square 2, above and to the right of where you came up. Begin your second stitch in square 3, directly below where you went down. When you reach the end of a row, turn the canvas upside down and work the next row from left to right.

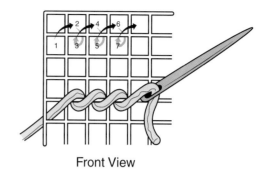

Front View

How to overstitch

Overstitching is used to finish the raw edges of a needlework project. Push your needle up through square 1. Loop the yarn over the edge of the canvas and come up again through square 2.

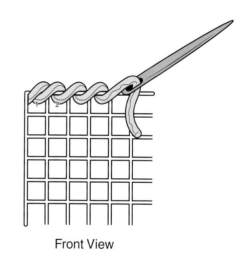

Front View

How to finish a row

When you reach the end of your row, or if you run out of yarn in the row you're stitching, complete your stitch at the back of the canvas. Slip your needle between the canvas and the yarn. Pull the thread tight under four or five stitches. Trim your yarn. Avoid using knots.

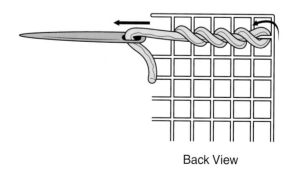

Back View

1 Draw a line across the canvas on the plastic between the tenth and eleventh rows of squares, counting from the top. Draw another line between the thirtieth and thirty-first rows.

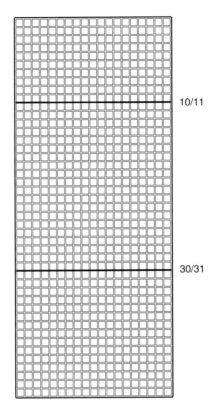

10/11

30/31

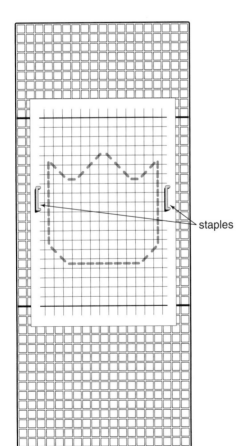

staples

2 Trace or photocopy one of the patterns at the top of page 45. Center it between the lines and staple the paper to the canvas.

3 Use a running stitch to outline the pattern in blue, sewing through the paper and the canvas. Cut or tear away the paper when you finish. Use slant stitches to fill in the pattern with pink.

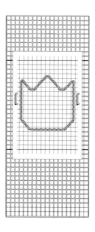

4 Finish the top and bottom edges with overstitching in blue.

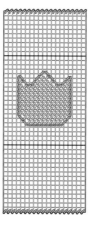

5 Still using blue, work a row of slant stitches to cover each line you drew in step 1.

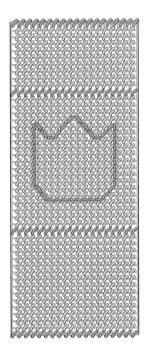

6 Switch to green yarn. Fill in the remaining canvas with slant stitches.

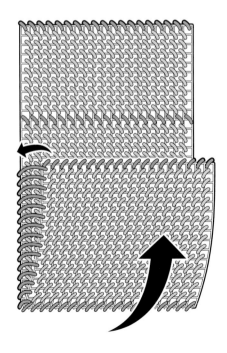

7 Bend up the bottom part of the canvas on the blue line. Using blue yarn, overstitch the edges together to create a purse. Continue overstitching to the top of the canvas. Repeat on the other side.

▲**8** Fold the top flap down at the blue line. Find the center of the flap and sew on one part of your snap with yarn or thread that matches your purse. Line up the other half of the snap on the front of the purse and sew it in place.

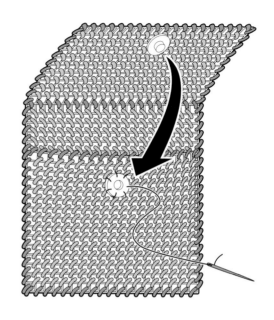

▲**9** Next you'll make two tassels. For each tassel, wind a strand of yarn 15 times around the piece of cardboard. Slide a piece of yarn between the cardboard and the bundle and tie the top of the bundle tightly. Cut the bottom of the yarn bundle open and remove the yarn from the cardboard. Tie a piece of yarn tightly around the top. Cut the bottom ends of the yarn evenly. Sew the tassels to the bottom corners of the purse.

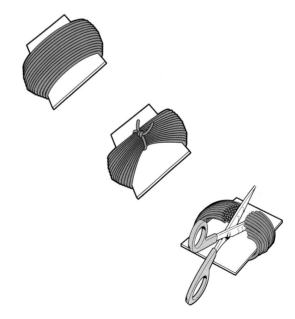

10 Finally, make a pom-pom for the flap of your purse. Wind the yarn 25 times around the cardboard. Slide the bundle off the cardboard and tie it tightly around the middle, making a bunch of loops at the top and bottom. Cut through the loops and trim the pom-pom to the size you want. Sew it to the purse.

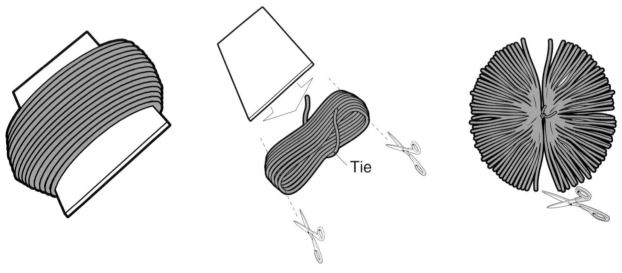

Tie

WHAT ELSE YOU CAN DO

Other Stitches: By changing the lengths of some stitches, you can create different textures. In one row, the stitches could go over two bars instead of one. In another row, the single stitches and double stitches might alternate. Experiment to come up with other styles.

Design Your Own: Design other needlework pictures. Draw strong outlines to fill with stitches. Or choose a geometric pattern made up of stripes or triangles.

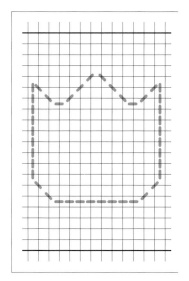

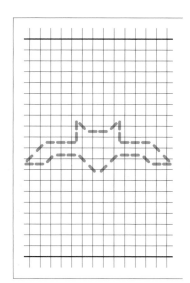

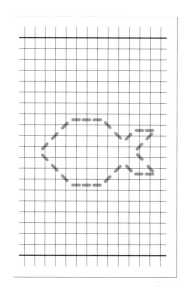

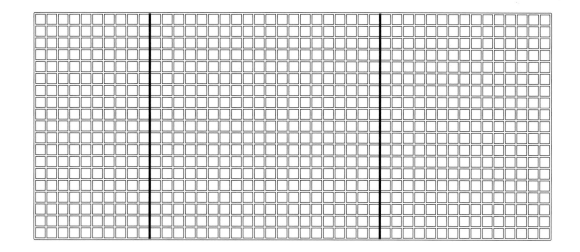

Wheat Straw Pictures

With toothpicks, glue, and paint, you can decorate a box using the same techniques as Chinese wheat straw artists.

DECORATING WITH WHEAT STRAW

In the northern part of China, people grow wheat as their main food. During the winter, when farmwork is light, families have time for hobbies. Some Chinese families find a use for the wheat straw, or dried stalks, left at the end of the harvest. They use it to decorate wooden boxes and greeting cards.

Wheat straw pictures , such as this bird (left) and tiger (above), often have elaborate detail.

TECHNIQUE

Chinese people might dye the straw different colors for the birds, flowers, or other designs on the picture. When you look at wheat straw pictures, you may be surprised that tiny pieces of straw can be lined up so exactly. Artisans make these complex patterns by gluing the straws onto a piece of paper and then cutting the straw and paper together into the necessary shapes.

HOW-TO PROJECT

Since wheat straw is not easily available in most places, you can substitute flat toothpicks to decorate a box.

1 On a scrap of paper, spread glue over an area about 2 inches by 2 inches. Put toothpicks close together on the paper, alternating their wide and narrow ends at the top and bottom. Make seven squares and let them dry.

> **You need:**
>
> Paper
> White glue
> Flat toothpicks
> Strong scissors
> Pencil
> Ruler
> Red, yellow, and green poster
>   paints
> Paintbrush
> A cardboard or wooden box

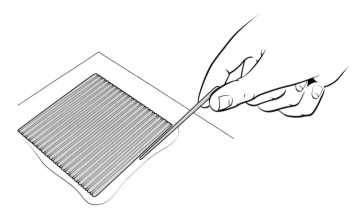

2 Cut away the paper around the glued toothpicks. Use the ruler to draw lines across the top and the bottom, 2 inches apart. Cut on the lines to remove the bumpy edges of the toothpick squares.

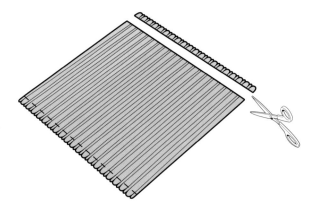

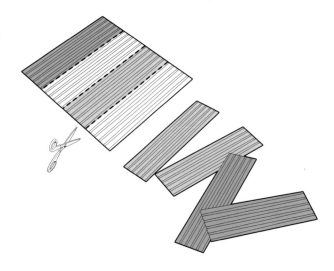

3 Paint the squares. Make two each in red, yellow, and green, or in any three colors you want. Leave one square unpainted. Let them all dry. Cut each square into four ½-inch-wide strips.

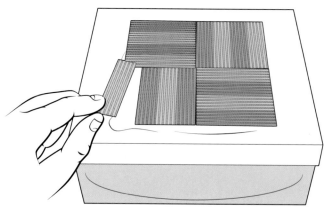

4 Make a mark in the middle of the box top. Arrange the red and yellow strips in a checkerboard pattern. Glue them down one by one.

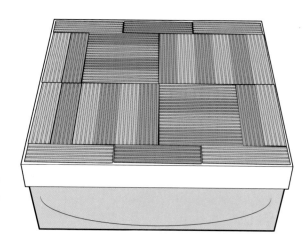

5 Fill in the outside with green and unpainted strips. Cut them to the sizes you need.

Picture Scrolls

For a different way to display a drawing, try mounting it Chinese-style on a scroll.

PAINTING AND CALLIGRAPHY

For more than a thousand years, Chinese artists have painted on long pieces of silk and paper. Traditional subjects include plants, landscapes, and calligraphy (fancy writing). Modern-day painters show these traditional subjects as well as scenes from everyday life and current events.

Instead of putting their paintings in frames, Chinese artists usually mount their work on scrolls. Mounting a painting on a scroll is a special craft.

Some scrolls don't have any pictures. Chinese people feel that calligraphy is as decorative as painting.

Unlike English, which has an alphabet, Chinese writing is made up of thousands of characters. A word may be represented by a single character or by a combination of two or three characters. Families often decorate their homes with tall posters expressing a favorite saying or poem. The writing may have been done by an artist known for his or her beautiful script. More characters appear on page 57.

 happy

 sun

 book

TECHNIQUE

Traditionally, Chinese artists paint with watercolors and black ink. They use soft brushes with pointed tips. The artist takes a finished painting to an expert scroll mounter. He or she selects paper of the texture and color best suited for a background. The scroll mounter cuts the background and glues the painting on, pasting it only at the four corners. He or she attaches a wooden roller to the bottom of the scroll and a strip of wood to the top. The scroll mounter finishes by adding silk strings for hanging or rolling up the scroll.

HOW-TO PROJECT

The rollers at the top and bottom of your hanging scroll are made of a wooden half-round—a dowel that is flat on the bottom and rounded on top. You can find a half-round at a hardware or home supply store. When you buy it, ask to have it cut into two 9-inch lengths.

You need:

Two pieces of wooden half-round, ¾ inch wide, 9 inches long
Small paintbrush
Black poster or acrylic paint
A 6- by 16-inch piece of watercolor paper
Watercolor paints and paintbrush or colored markers
White glue
A piece of colored art paper, 8 inches wide, 24 inches long
Ruler
Scissors
Cord or ribbon

1 Paint the half-rounds black and let them dry.

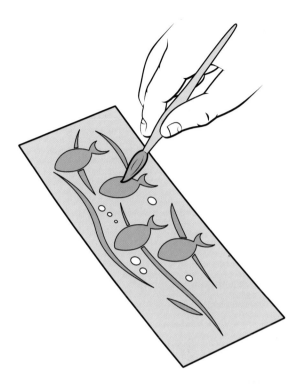

2 Paint your picture vertically on the watercolor paper. You can paint an outdoor scene, a saying or poem, or anything else you like.

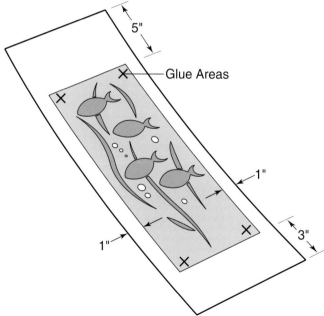

5"

Glue Areas

1"

1"

3"

3 Glue the painting to the piece of colored paper. Leave a margin of 5 inches at the top, 3 inches at the bottom, and 1 inch on either side. Put glue only at the four corners of your painting.

4 Glue the wooden half-rounds, flat side down, to the front of the scroll at the top and the bottom.

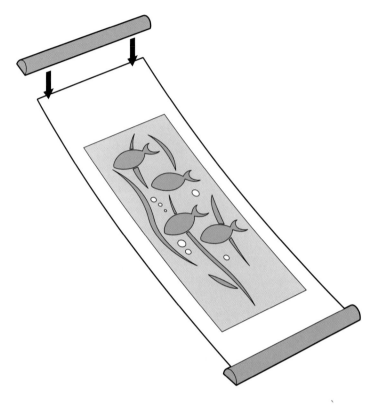

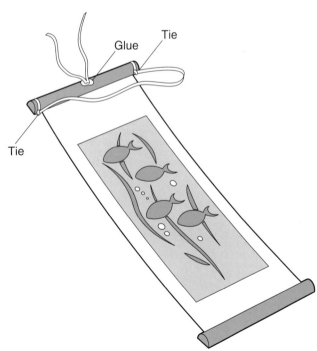

5 Cut a piece of cord or ribbon 8 inches long. Tie the ends of the cord to the right and left sides of the top half-round. Cut another 8-inch piece of cord. Fold it in half. Glue the middle of the cord to the center of the top half-round.

6 Hang up the scroll. When you want to take it someplace or put it away, roll it up from the bottom and tie it with the piece of ribbon glued to the center of the half-round.

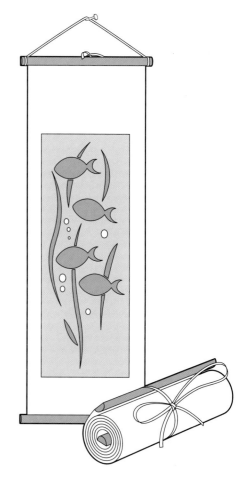

WHAT ELSE YOU CAN DO

Symbols: Chinese artists often paint pictures that have symbolic meanings in their culture. Chrysanthemums represent fall, which is the time of the year when they bloom. Peonies mean love and affection, and they are the sign of spring. The bat stands for good fortune. The beautiful feathers of the peacock are a sign of high rank. Goldfish stand for wealth, dragonflies mean summer, and a rooster is a symbol for protecting the home. You can look up other Chinese symbols or paint figures that symbolize something to you.

Horizontal Scroll: Tell a story in several scenes painted side by side on a horizontal hand scroll. Hand scrolls are meant not for hanging but for reading like a book. Some Chinese hand scrolls are very long, and people view only small sections at a time. The wooden rollers at both ends keep the hand scroll stretched flat while it is open.

見 有 行 友 山 宅 読

see   have   go   friend   mountain   house   read

METRIC CONVERSION CHART

If you want to use the metric system, convert measurements using the chart on the right. Because fractions can be hard to work with, round all metric measurements to the nearest whole number.

when you know:	multiply by:	to find:
Length		
inches	25.00	millimeters
inches	2.54	centimeters
feet	30.00	centimeters
feet	.30	meters
yards	.91	meters
miles	1.61	kilometers
Volume		
teaspoons	5.00	milliliters
tablespoons	15.00	milliliters
fluid ounces	30.00	milliliters
cups	0.24	liters
pints	0.47	liters
quarts	0.95	liters
gallons	3.80	liters
Weight		
ounces	28.00	grams
pounds	0.45	kilograms

GLOSSARY

artisan: A person who is very skilled at making crafts

bamboo: A tall, treelike plant that grows in warm parts of China. People build houses and make utensils from bamboo. They also cook the plant's young shoots.

calligraphy: Beautiful, decorative writing

ceramics: The art of creating objects made of baked clay

culture: The customs, ideas, and traditions of a certain group of people. Culture includes religious celebrations, arts and crafts, folktales, costumes, and food.

embroidery: The art of using colored thread to stitch pictures onto pieces of cloth

endangered species: A kind of plant or animal that is in danger of dying out

folklore: Traditional stories, sayings, and customs that are passed down from generation to generation

natural resources: Materials, such as plants, water, stone, or metals, that people take from the land and make into useful objects

porcelain: A special kind of very fine, thin, white ceramic object, or the kind of clay from which it is made

province: A section of a country, similar to a state

stencil: Paper or other material on which a cutout design has been made

zodiac: A group of twelve sets of stars. People imagine an animal or other shape in each set of stars. Each shape, or sign, rises into the night sky for a period of time. Traditional beliefs say that the zodiac sign can affect people and events during that time.

READ MORE ABOUT CHINA

Fiction & Folktales

Chang, Margaret, and Raymond Chang. *The Beggar's Magic: A Chinese Tale*. New York: Margaret K. McElderry Books for Young Readers, 1997.

Chang, Margaret Scrogin, and Raymond Chang. *Da Wei's Treasure: A Chinese Tale*. New York: Margaret K. McElderry Books for Young Readers, 1999.

Gao, R. L. *Adventures of Monkey King*. Monterey, CA: Victory Press, 1989.

McCully, Emily Arnold. *Beautiful Warrior: The Legend of the Nun's Kung Fu*. New York: Scholastic, 1998.

Yep, Laurence. *The Rainbow People*. New York: HarperCollins, 1992.

Zhang, Song Nan. *The Ballad of Mulan*. Union City, CA: Pan Asian Publications, 1998.

Nonfiction

Ancient China. The Nature Company Discovery Library. Alexandria, VA: Time-Life Books, 1996.

Baldwin, Robert F. *Daily Life in Ancient and Modern Beijing.* Minneapolis: Runestone Press, 1999.

Demi. *Happy New Year! Kung-hsi Fa-ts'ai!* New York: Crown Publishers, Inc., 1997.

Goldstein, Peggy. *Long Is a Dragon: Chinese Writing for Children.* Berkeley, CA: Pacific View Press, 1991.

Haskins, Jim. *Count Your Way through China.* Minneapolis: Carolrhoda Books, Inc., 1987.

Helmer, Diana Star. *Panda Bears.* New York: Powerkids Press, 1997.

Krach, Maywan Shen. *D is for Doufu: An Alphabet Book of Chinese Culture.* Arcadia, CA: Shen's Books, 1997.

Pitkänen, Matti A. *The Children of China.* Minneapolis: Carolrhoda Books, Inc., 1990.

Riehecky, Janet. *China.* Globe-trotters Club. Minneapolis: Carolrhoda Books, Inc., 1998.

Williams, Suzanne. *Made in China: Ideas and Inventions from Ancient China.* Berkeley, CA: Pacific View Press, 1996.

INDEX

ABOUT THE AUTHOR

Florence Temko is an internationally known author of more than 40 books on world folkcrafts and paper arts. She has traveled in 31 countries, gaining much of her skill first-hand. Ms. Temko shows her enthusiasm for crafts through simple, inventive adaptations of traditional arts and crafts projects. She has presented hundreds of hands-on programs in schools and museums, including the Metropolitan Museum of Art in New York City and the Children's Museum in Boston. She lives in San Diego, California, where she is a consultant for the Mingei International Museum.

ACKNOWLEDGMENTS

The photographs in this book are reproduced with the permission of:

Turkish Republic, Ministry of Culture and Tourism, p. 6 (left); Wilford Archaeology Laboratory, University of Minnesota, by Kathy Raskob/IPS, p. 6 (right); Nelson-Atkins Museum of Art, Kansas City, Missouri (Purchase: Nelson Trust), p. 7 (left); Freer Gallery of Art, Smithsonian Institution, p. 7 (right); Robert L. and Diane Wolfe, pp. 8, 9; IPS, pp. 12, 16, 22, 28, 32, 36, 46, 50; © Christopher Liu/ChinaStock, pp. 13, 23, 33 (all); © Liu Liqun/ChinaStock, p. 17 (left); © Dennis Cox/ChinaStock, pp. 17 (right), © Liu Xiaoyang/ChinaStock, 37, 51; pp. 29, 47 (both).

Cover photo by IPS.

The map on page 11 is by John Erste. The illustrations on pages 2, 11, 23, 29, 51, and 57 (bottom row) are by Laura Westlund.